MW00698501

Wishes
for you,
Graduate

by
Marianne Richmond

Wishes for you, Graduate

Marianne Richmond Studios, Inc.
420 N. 5th Street, Suite 840
Minneapolis, MN 55401
www.mariannerichmond.com

ISBN 0-9763101-3-9

Illustrations by Marianne Richmond

Book design by Meg Anderson

Printed in China

Second Printing

TO

FROM

Date

Congrats Graduate!

Did you think this
day would ever come?
And now, what's next?

As you begin your next adventure,
I wish to send with you my wishes...

I wish you guts.

Challenge your ability by
trying something new...
even if you're scared
or nervous
or about to throw up.

I
wish
you
a
generous
heart.

Share your time
and resources
with others,

don't expect
anything in return,

and watch your
good fortune grow.

I wish you
a playful spirit.

It's forever "cool" to dance,
     master the monkey bars,
spin a cartwheel,
          wish upon a star,
hug your mom or dad,
          befriend a child, or
hand out Halloween candy.

I wish you humility.

One of the greatest gifts you
can give is to be genuinely
interested in another's life.
Ask questions and listen
more than you talk.

I wish you patience
with others.

Seems like
everything takes
longer than you hope.

Friends let you down.

A boss can be
downright annoying.

Traffic is crazy.

People are rude.

Take a deep breath
before you blow.

I wish you patience with yourself, too.

Give your all _and_ give
yourself a break.

If you finish 3rd place
when you want 1st...
go easy on yourself
while you improve.

I wish you determination.

Some things will come easy.

A lot won't.

Whatever your goal, remind yourself why it's important...

and keep going....

I wish you great friendships.

Surround yourself with loving, supportive, funny friends and tell them how much you like and appreciate them!

I wish you a great sense of humor.

If you can find the fun in life,
you'll find the journey
much more entertaining!

I wish you an opinion.
What do you think about
this or that?

Do you agree or disagree?
Speak up (nicely)...
and state your case!

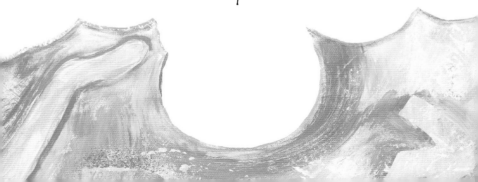

I wish you
an open mind.

Okay, so you
have your opinion.

But, be open
to other's ideas,
ways, customs,
and preferences.

Acceptance
cultivates
kindness.

I wish you

common sense.

When faced
with situations,
decisions,
quandaries and
questions, consult
your experiences
and instincts
and try to
respond with
good judgment.

I wish you
curiosity.

Keep asking,

keep trying,

keep learning,

keep living.

I wish you honesty.
It's hard (sometimes)
to tell AND hear
the truth.

Do it with gentleness and tact,
however, and you will
gain respect, win friends
and feel better about yourself.

I wish you self-respect.

Do you like you?

Do you know your limits,
values and absolutes?

A strong "moral compass" will be
your ultimate guide through life.

I wish you joyfulness.

Laugh often.
Plan surprises.
Be spontaneous.
Tell jokes.
Be silly.

Lastly, I wish you luck.

For all the planning, striving,
hoping and learning we do —
there's no substitute for
great timing and pure luck!

Congrats, Graduate!

A gifted author and artist, Marianne Richmond shares
her creations with millions of people worldwide
through her delightful books, cards, and giftware.
In addition to the *Simply Said...* and *Smartly Said...*
gift book series, she has written and illustrated five
additional books: **The Gift of an Angel,
The Gift of a Memory, Hooray for You!,
The Gifts of Being Grand, I Love You So....,
My Shoes Take Me Where I Want to Go,
Dear Daughter** and **Dear Son**

To learn more about Marianne's products, please visit
www.mariannerichmond.com.